A LOOK AT CHEMISTRY

MOLECULES

BY KENNON O'MARA

Gareth Stevens
PUBLISHING

Please visit our website, www.garethstevens.com. For a free color catalog of all our high-quality books, call toll free 1-800-542-2595 or fax 1-877-542-2596.

Library of Congress Cataloging-in-Publication Data

Names: O'Mara, Kennon, author.
Title: Molecules / Kennon O'Mara.
Description: New York : Gareth Stevens Publishing, [2019] | Series: A look at chemistry | Includes index.
Identifiers: LCCN 2018014329| ISBN 9781538230121 (library bound) | ISBN 9781538231425 (pbk.) | ISBN 9781538233290 (6 pack)
Subjects: LCSH: Molecules--Juvenile literature. | Atoms--Juvenile literature.
Classification: LCC QC173.16 .O43 2019 | DDC 539/.6--dc23
LC record available at https://lccn.loc.gov/2018014329

First Edition

Published in 2019 by
Gareth Stevens Publishing
111 East 14th Street, Suite 349
New York, NY 10003

Designer: Reann Nye
Editor: Therese Shea

Photo credits: Series art Marina Sun/Shutterstock.com; cover Egorov Artem/Shutterstock.com; pp. 5, 25 Triff/Shutterstock.com; p. 7 Raksak Raksa/Shutterstock.com; p. 27 HandmadePictures/Shutterstock.com; p. 29 Carol Mellema/Shutterstock.com.

Printed in the United States of America

CPSIA compliance information: Batch #CW19GS: For further information contact Gareth Stevens, New York, New York at 1-800-542-2595.

CONTENTS

Words in the glossary appear in **bold** type the first time they are used in the text.

LET'S GET TOGETHER

Atoms are the tiny building blocks of all matter on Earth and in the **universe**! There may be **trillions** of atoms in the tiniest bit of matter you can see. When they connect to each other, atoms make groups called molecules.

MAKE THE GRADE

Atoms aren't usually found
by themselves.

INTO ELEMENTS

Molecules make up the elements. Elements are **substances** that can't be broken down into simpler substances. However, as molecules, they join with other molecules to build matter. Hydrogen, carbon, oxygen, and gold are just a few elements you may know.

TIN

MAKE THE GRADE

The molecules in each element contain only one kind of atom. For example, pure tin contains only tin atoms.

The molecules of some
elements have just one
atom. For example, helium
molecules contain only
one atom. Some, such as
hydrogen, nitrogen, and
chlorine, have only two
atoms bonded together. Pure
elements have only one kind
of molecule containing one
kind of atom.

NITROGEN MOLECULE

N

N

WHAT'S A COMPOUND?

Molecules that contain atoms of more than one kind of element are called compounds. When atoms of different elements join to become a compound, the elements can lose their **properties**. The elemental gases hydrogen and oxygen bond to become a liquid—water!

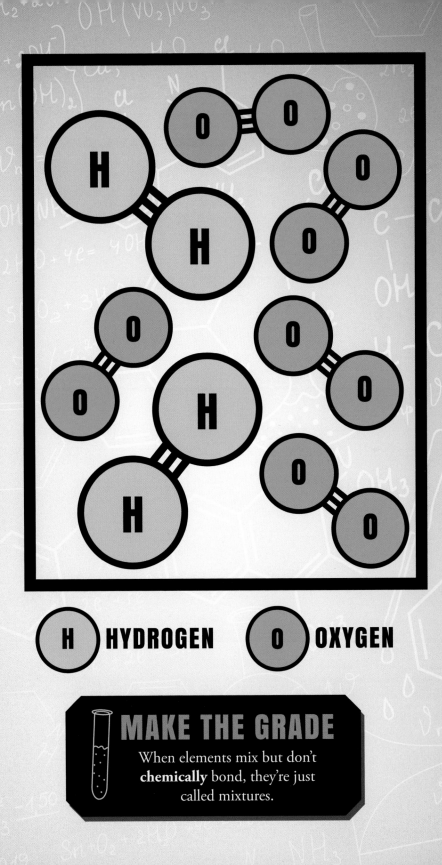

H HYDROGEN   O OXYGEN

MAKE THE GRADE

When elements mix but don't **chemically** bond, they're just called mixtures.

AMAZING ATOMS

To understand how molecules and compounds form, you need to know about atoms. Atoms are made up of small **particles** called protons, neutrons, and electrons. Protons and neutrons are found at the center of the atom, called its nucleus. Electrons travel around the nucleus.

ATOM

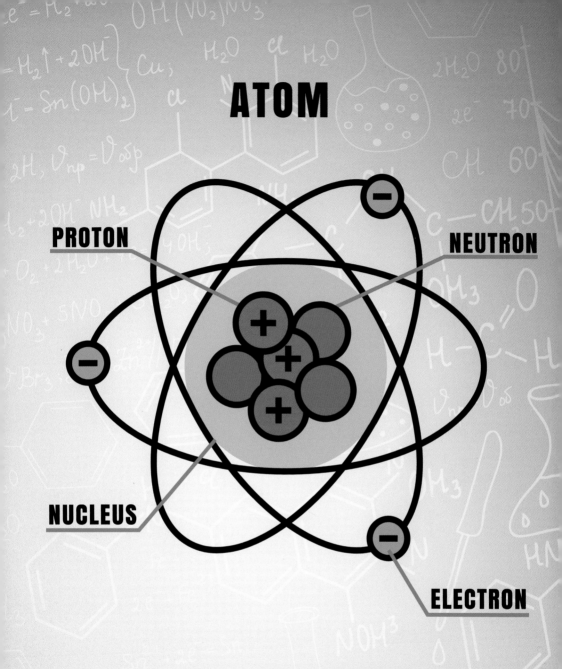

PROTON

NEUTRON

NUCLEUS

ELECTRON

MAKE THE GRADE

Much of an atom is empty space!

Electrons are located in spaces called shells around the nucleus. Electrons have a negative electric charge, while protons have a positive charge. Opposite charges **attract**, so the electrons are attracted to the protons. This keeps the electrons in place.

 **PROTON**
POSITIVE CHARGE

 **ELECTRON**
NEGATIVE CHARGE

 **NEUTRON**
NO CHARGE

OPPOSITE CHARGES ATTRACT

MAKE THE GRADE

Neutrons have no electric charge.

LET'S BOND

The outermost electron shell controls whether the atom will bond with other atoms to create a molecule or compound. There are three ways an atom forms a bond with another atom. The first is **transferring** an electron to another atom.

IONIC BOND

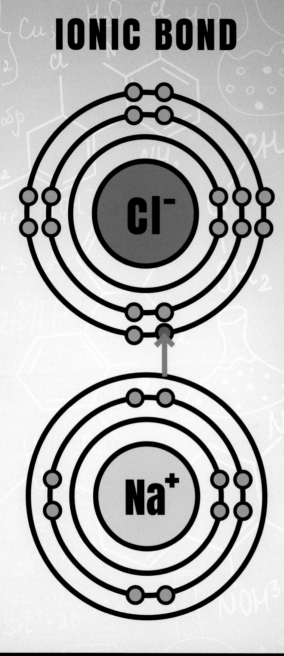

Cl⁻

Na⁺

MAKE THE GRADE

The atom that loses an electron becomes positively charged, while the atom that gains the electron becomes negatively charged. The bond between them is called ionic.

Electrons can be shared
between two atoms. This
forms a strong connection
called a covalent bond.
Electrons can also be shared
among many atoms of metal
elements. The electrons don't
become fixed to one atom
but move among them. This
is metallic bonding.

COVALENT BOND

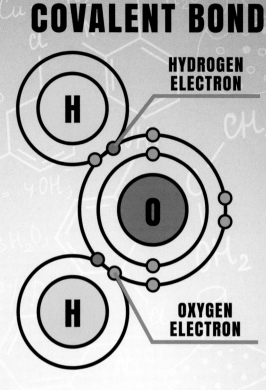

HYDROGEN ELECTRON

H

O

OXYGEN ELECTRON

H

METALLIC BOND

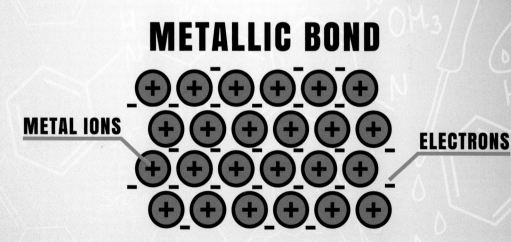

METAL IONS

ELECTRONS

MAKE THE GRADE

Diamonds are formed by covalent bonds between carbon atoms.

19

COUNTLESS COMPOUNDS!

There are 118 known elements—and 118 different kinds of atoms. However, scientists have discovered there are many millions of compounds! Compounds can be made of many different kinds of atoms as well as different numbers of atoms.

VITAMIN C COMPOUND

⬤ CARBON   ⬤ OXYGEN   ⬤ HYDROGEN

MAKE THE GRADE

Scientists sometimes shorten the names of
elements. For example, "H" is hydrogen,
"O" is oxygen, and "C" is carbon.

Some compounds have names, like the compound **caffeine** does. However, they may be called by their chemical **formula**, too. A chemical formula tells us the elements in a compound as well as the number of each kind of atom.

CAFFEINE COMPOUND

○ **CARBON**   ○ **OXYGEN**

○ **NITROGEN**   ○ **HYDROGEN**

MAKE THE GRADE

The properties of a compound
depend on how the atoms
are arranged.

Let's look at the chemical formula of water: H_2O. This tells us there are two hydrogen (H) atoms and one oxygen (O) atom. Water—or H_2O—covers more than 70 percent of Earth's surface. This compound is needed for life to exist!

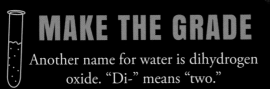

MAKE THE GRADE

Another name for water is dihydrogen
oxide. "Di-" means "two."

There are different kinds of salt, but table salt is a compound you eat! Next time you want some salt at the dinner table, you can use this molecule's chemical name: "Please pass the sodium chloride!"

The chemical formula for table salt is NaCl. There are no numbers in it, so it has one atom of sodium (Na) and one atom of chloride (Cl).

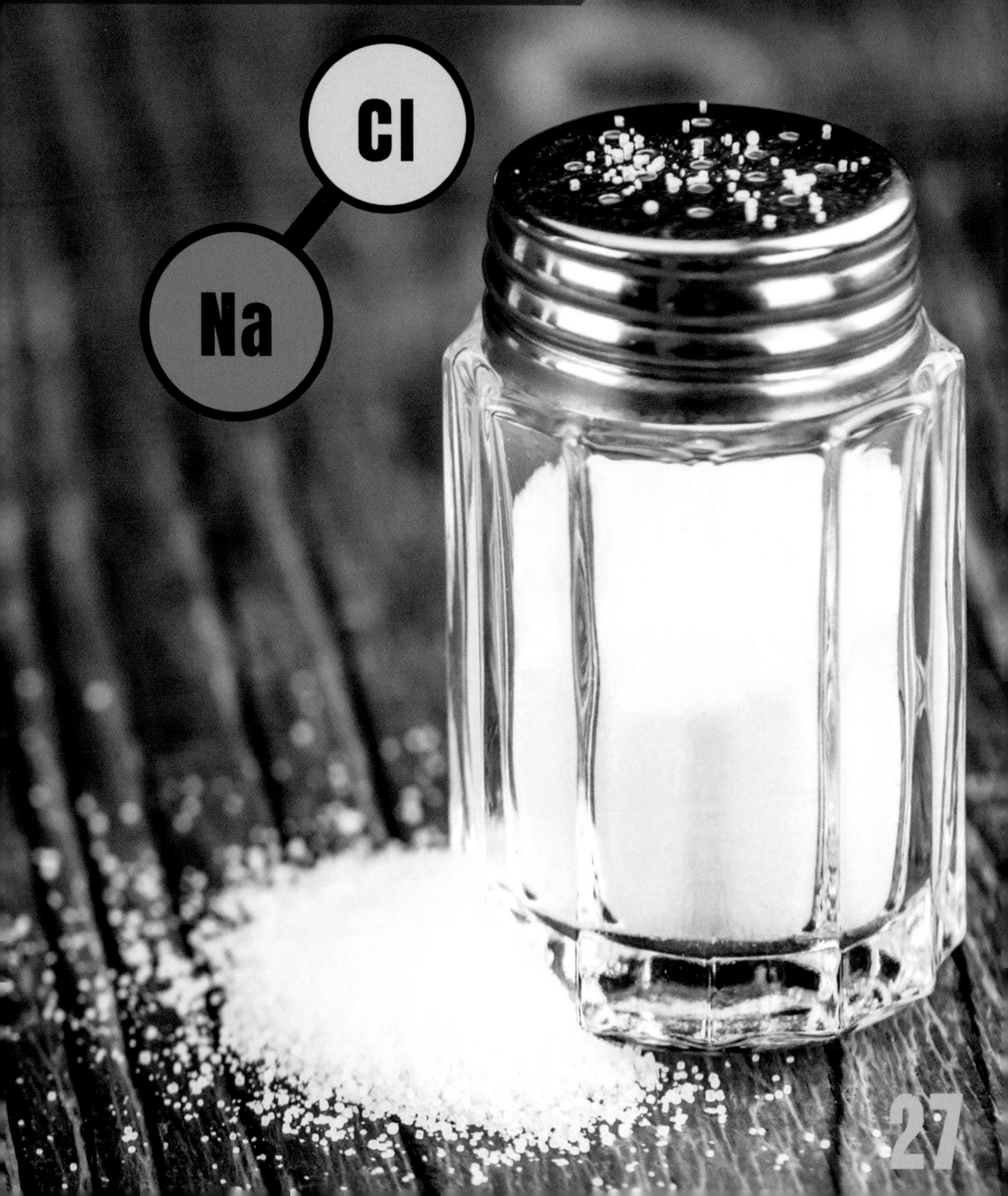

Cl

Na

There are many other compounds you know well, but you probably don't think of them as compounds. Sucrose is a sugar people bake with. It's a compound of carbon, hydrogen, and oxygen. Without compounds, we wouldn't have cookies! Molecules are amazing!

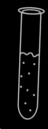

MAKE THE GRADE

The chemical formula for sucrose is $C_{12}H_{22}O_{11}$. It has 12 atoms of carbon, 22 atoms of hydrogen, and 11 atoms of oxygen.

MORE KEY COMPOUNDS

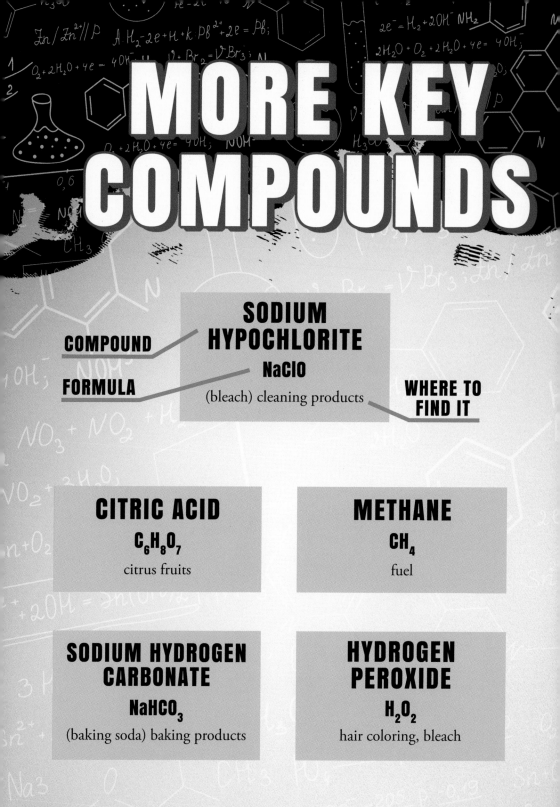

COMPOUND

FORMULA

SODIUM HYPOCHLORITE

NaClO

(bleach) cleaning products

WHERE TO FIND IT

CITRIC ACID

$C_6H_8O_7$

citrus fruits

METHANE

CH_4

fuel

SODIUM HYDROGEN CARBONATE

$NaHCO_3$

(baking soda) baking products

HYDROGEN PEROXIDE

H_2O_2

hair coloring, bleach

GLOSSARY

attract: to draw nearer

caffeine: a substance found in coffee and tea that makes you feel more awake

chemically: having to do with matter that can be mixed with other matter to cause changes

formula: a series of letters, numbers, and symbols showing the chemicals that a compound is made of

particle: a very small piece of something

property: a special quality or feature of something

substance: a certain kind of matter

transfer: to move something from one place to another

trillion: the number 1,000,000,000,000

universe: everything that exists

FOR MORE INFORMATION

BOOKS

Lepora, Nathan. *Inside Atoms and Molecules*. New York, NY: Marshall Cavendish Benchmark, 2010.

Maurer, Tracy. *Atoms and Molecules*. Vero Beach, FL: Rourke Educational Media, 2013.

WEBSITES

Molecules
www.dkfindout.com/us/science/solids-liquids-and-gases/molecules/
Find out about some well-known molecules here.

Molecules
www.ducksters.com/science/molecules.php
Read about the molecules that make up the sweet treat called sugar!

Publisher's note to educators and parents: Our editors have carefully reviewed these websites to ensure that they are suitable for students. Many websites change frequently, however, and we cannot guarantee that a site's future contents will continue to meet our high standards of quality and educational value. Be advised that students should be closely supervised whenever they access the internet.

INDEX